TO SAIL
NO MORE

Ian Buxton & Ben Warlow

THE RESERVE FLEET

There has always been a problem of achieving a sensible balance between the availability and requirement for both ships and men. In times of peace the needs are low, and in war they are great. If the steady state (of war or peace) persists, then levels settle and everyone is relatively happy. However, having the right numbers available at the outbreak of war rarely happens - hence most of the British ships engaged in the Armada were 'taken up from trade', and much the same occurred again at the time of the Falklands War. Equally, the ending of wars leaves many men and ships surplus. Sailors are cast out onto the streets, and ships laid up in creeks. The period between the two World Wars was relatively short, but many ships were scrapped, some of which could have served in 1939. Indeed several ships were recalled from the clutches of the breakers at the last minute. The ending of the Second World War, heralding a period of at least 50 years of relative peace, was an interesting period, as there were many ships and the lessons of a too eager "Peace in our time" and "War to end all wars" attitude were still clear in the memory of a Navy which had had a hard struggle, especially in the early years when shortages of ships of all descriptions had been grievously felt.

Before the Second World War drew to its close, the Royal Navy was already paying off some old ships to provide crews for its newer vessels. These old ships were laid up pending a decision as to their future. The Reserve Fleet, which had been mobilised in 1939, was reinstated on 15 January 1944. The Admiral's flag was hoisted in the battleship MALAYA. She was in care and maintenance on the Clyde, but was to be recommissioned later that year for bombardment duties.

Ships of the Reserve Fleet were put into one of three categories: a) new construction ships for which crews were not available; b) ships which would be required; and c) ships unlikely to be needed. In 1947 the categories were redefined. Operational Reserve 1 comprised ships required in a future emergency, maintained (including docking etc.) for operational service and at 14 days' notice. Operational Reserve 2 were also ships needed for a future emergency and at 14 days' notice, but which would require docking etc. to make them fully operational. Supplementary Reserve ships would only be required in a future emergency and would need a minor refit for limited operational service. Extended Reserve were ships required in a future emergency but which would need an extensive refit prior to even limited operational duty. Disposal List were ships no longer required. This was revised again in October 1949 to Operational Reserve (A), Supplementary Reserve (B), Extended Reserve (C) and Disposal List (Z).

A further redefinition took place in 1952 - Category A ships were to be fit for service in 3 months, if possible at 30 days' notice; Category B ships were those required for operational service, but not until after ships in Category A. Category C ships were to be preserved for future use after full mobilisation. Category Z ships were those no longer required. This grading was amended slightly over the next few years, with Roman numerals replacing letters, i.e. Category A became Class I.

In August 1944 there were 27 ships in the Reserve Fleet; this number rose to 434 by the end of 1945. There were also about 60 submarines in reserve, which were under the control of Flag Officer Submarines. Although the older ships were broken up, in August 1947 there were 387 ships in the Reserve Fleet and 58 reserve submarines. In 1949 it was decided that some of these ships would be refitted by contract in commercial yards. By January 1950 the Reserve Fleet had reduced to 285 ships, with a further 42 submarines in reserve.

They were laid up in ports around the United Kingdom, and also at

Singapore and Malta. The Forth Area Reserve Fleet (HMS QUEENSFERRY) was closed in March 1950. That year the Korean War broke out and naval pensioners were called up to maintain the ships in reserve, ships in Categories A-C having skeleton crews. Refits were speeded up, and in March 1951 it was announced that 60 ships were being brought forward from the Reserve Fleet.

All ships for reserve, except those for Category Z, carried out trials prior to being laid up. Ships in Categories A and B retained most of their stores and ammunition, whilst ships in Category C were destored. Ships in Category Z were both destored and de-equipped. In 1952 it was decided to lay up ships at commercial ports. This was partly an economy measure, as alongside berths could be used, providing better access for the skeleton crews as well as shore power supplies; and partly as a dispersal measure lest there be a nuclear attack on dockyard ports.

These ships were to be preserved by 'de-humidification'. In this process the relative humidity in the ship was reduced to between 25 and 30 per cent and the ship sealed, thus slowing down the process of deterioration of the structure and fittings inside the ship. Air was drawn into the ship by a fan placed high in the ship, and passed through a desiccant before circulation inside the ship and escaping through set vents. Guns, equipment and openings (like funnels) were covered by netting on which plastic was sprayed, a process called "Kooncoting".

The commercial ports chosen for these reserve ships were Cardiff, Penarth and West Hartlepool, followed by Barrow-in-Furness, Lisahally (Londonderry), North Shields, Barry, Llanelly (landing craft), and Portchester (minesweepers). Gibraltar came into use in 1953. Meanwhile the Reserve Division at Sheerness (HMS MINERVA) was closed in April 1953, and that at Harwich (HMS MARS) in 1954. The former British Overseas Airways Base at Hythe was purchased and converted as a commissioning base for minesweepers (HMS DILIGENCE). Newly delivered coastal minesweepers which were not needed for service immediately were decked over like Noah's Ark and laid up on Southampton Water.

During this period the Reserve Fleet was put on a firmer footing, and the problems caused by its rapid inception at the end of the war tackled. Regular maintenance and drydockings were carried out, often in commercial repair yards. Fourteen of the ships attended the Coronation Review at Spithead in June 1953. In 1955 trials were carried out to bring forward ships from dehumidification to a fully operational status (Operation SLEEPING BEAUTY), the first being the frigate EGLINTON. One exercise was conducted using RNVR officers and men.

In 1956 there was a review of the cost of maintaining modern ships at the high states of readiness required lest a thermo-nuclear war should occur. It was decided that only a small number of ships should be maintained to this standard, and that the other ships of the Reserve Fleet would either be sold to friendly navies or disposed of at the end of their useful lives. As a result the Reserve Fleet dwindled in size, concentrating again in the dockyard ports. (HMS ORION at Devonport and HMS BELLEROPHON at Portsmouth). The Clyde Division (HMS JUPITER) closed in September 1957, with the battleships and carriers going for scrap. Ships were withdrawn from North Shields in 1955; Llanelly in 1956; Penarth, Barry and Cardiff in 1960; West Hartlepool in 1962 and Barrow-in-Furness and Lisahally in 1964.

The Flag Officer Reserve Fleet was replaced by a Commodore Reserve Ships in 1960. In 1961 ships were either classified as being in Operational Reserve or on the Disposal List. The latter category was sub-divided into those ships for sale and those for scrap. The Commodore's post became a Captain's in 1969. The Portsmouth Reserve Fleet paid off in 1971, a Stand-By Squadron being formed at Chatham in 1970 but was disbanded in December 1982. Ships that are no longer required are now disposed of by sale to friendly navies, as targets or by breaking up.

Fountain Lake between Portsmouth Dockyard and Whale Island provided berths for Reserve Fleet ships. Furthest left is the cruiser LIVERPOOL, then MAURITIUS, the Daring class destroyer DAINTY and Type 15 frigate VERULAM. The three Algerine minesweepers are WATERWITCH (nearest), ACUTE and JEWEL. Astern of them are the Type 15 RAPID (nearest), Type 16 TUSCAN and LOCH TRALAIG shortly before she was moved to Hartlepool. The three destroyers are FINISTERRE (right), CAPRICE and TRAFALGAR. The Admiralty Floating Dock in the background is AFD 11, which arrived from Southampton in 1939. The photograph was probably taken in the spring of 1955.

Flotilla leader DUNCAN was laid up in June 1945 at Barrow-in-Furness after arduous service in the Western Approaches. She was handed over to BISCO (the acronym for the British Iron & Steel Corporation) the following month, but then lay untouched for over 3 years. She is seen here moving from her lay-up berth to T W Ward's Devonshire Dock demolition berth on 1 February 1949. Ward's also had a berth in the Ramsden Dock, although the stripped down hulks were beached for final demolition in the Walney Channel.

Although the original photo of Fareham Creek off Hardway in Portsmouth Harbour is not dated, the presence of monitor ABERCROMBIE (centre left) puts it before December 1954 when she went for scrap. The Dido class cruiser ARGONAUT is alongside her, while her two sisters (bottom left) are SIRIUS (nearest) and PHOEBE. The two other Didos top centre are DIDO (right) and CLEOPATRA. As the latter did not arrive at Portsmouth until October 1953, this sets an earliest date to the photo. The lone submarine in the foreground is probably SERAPH, while astern of her are probably JUTLAND and COWDRAY. The 1903-built coal depot with its Temperley transporters dominates the middle of the creek, while the single frigate to its right is the Hunt class BRECON. The unusual four legged pontoon is one of the Mulberry harbour spud pierheads. The pendant number D168 on the left hand destroyer identifies her as CRISPIN, with probably MYNGS alongside.

Malta's Lazaretto Creek shows both operational and Reserve Fleet vessels. The latter comprised mainly minesweeping and smaller patrol types, with A/S vessels concentrated in the UK. Five minesweeping Isles class trawlers (IMERSAY, SHILLAY, TOCOGAY, TRODDAY and VALLAY) are at the near right, with a small minelayer outboard, probably MINER 6. The four Algerine ocean minesweepers in Class 1 reserve (as it was then called) are FIERCE, ROWENA, STORMCLOUD and SYLVIA. The three operational Algerines in the centre with awnings spread are probably RIFLEMAN, PLUCKY and CHAMELEON of the 2nd Minesweeping Squadron. The depot ship at the left looks like TYNE, which would date the photograph at April 1954, when she was en route from the Indian Ocean to the UK as a HQ ship. The Black Swan astern of her could be MAGPIE which was in the 2nd Frigate Squadron based in the Med at the time. The vessels in the mid distance look like visiting Italian destroyers and minesweepers. Small craft laid up include fifteen motor launches in trots of three.

West Hartlepool was one of the dispersal ports chosen for the Reserve Fleet, the first ships arriving in 1952. This aerial view on 5 June 1957 looking north includes in the nearest L-shaped Swainson Dock three River class frigates, three Hunts and seven Seaward Defence Boats. In the Coal Dock at right are the same six Castles as Page 10, with astern of them LOCH ARKAIG (inboard), HIND, TANGANYIKA and MRC 1098. On the end of the jetty is the trawler SANDRAY. In the Jackson Dock between the two former groups are LOCH TRALAIG (inboard), TALYBONT and ESPIEGLE, with LOCH MORE partly visible behind the big warehouse. In the far corner of the further Union Dock are OBEDIENT (inboard), BLANKNEY and MARY ROSE, while the nearer trot of four are MARMION (inboard), ALBACORE, PROVIDENCE and MOON. Thirty-eight ships in all. [Turners Photography]

Thirty-one ships were berthed at Hartlepool on 8 April 1956. This view of the Coal Dock (where WARRIOR was restored) shows Isles class minesweeping trawler SANDRAY alongside Black Swan frigate HIND. Inboard is the headquarters ship LOCH ARKAIG which had arrived in 1952.

A trot of six Castle class frigates also at Hartlepool on 8 April 1956, whose sterns can be seen in the preceding photo. From left to right are: ALLINGTON CASTLE, then ALNWICK, FARNHAM, HADLEIGH (the first to be completed by corvette pioneer builders Smiths Dock on the Tees only ten miles away), DUMBARTON and LANCASTER CASTLEs. Gray's Dock Yard is in the left background, which drydocked the Reserve Fleet ships on a regular basis. All six Castles had gone to north-east breakers by 1960, each realising between £9600 and £11800 in net scrap proceeds after deducting all demolition costs.

Another view of the Coal Dock at Hartlepool, but sixteen months later than that on Pages 9-10. Here, on 18 August 1957, the only changes are the vessels lying on HIND (F39) and LOCH ARKAIG, now TANGANYIKA (arrived from Chatham in Operational Reserve) and MRC 1098. Maintenance & Repair Craft (MRC's) were Mark 3 Landing Craft (Tank) converted to mobile workshops.

Moored in the Hamoaze at Plymouth on 3 August 1956 are the destroyer ZEBRA and minesweeper POLARIS. The Parliamentary Select Committee on Estimates reported on the Reserve Fleet in Session 1957-58. ZEBRA was then on the Sales List available to friendly navies, but when MPs were taken round her, they were appalled at her dilapidated condition. They recommended that more such ships should be scrapped; ZEBRA went to Cashmore's yard at Newport in February 1959.

Ships in Operational Reserve were sometimes berthed in dockyard basins. Here at the end of the finger jetty in 5 Basin at Devonport on 4 August 1956 is the Type 16 anti-submarine frigate TERPSICHORE, recently converted from a destroyer by Thornycroft at Southampton. In the north-west corner (now occupied by the submarine refitting complex) are the bows of (left to right) the Type 15 frigate ROEBUCK, netlayer GUARDIAN and LST TRACKER (shortly to become a harbour accommodation vessel) and maintenance ship BERRY HEAD then serving as a living ship. The latter remained afloat for a further 34 years before being scrapped in Turkey in 1990.

13

Harwich had been used as a lay-up base soon after WW2, with trots of escort vessels in the estuary, but most of the vessels had gone by 28 September 1955 when this view was taken. The first trot shows three boom defence vessels PLANET, BARRHEAD and BARCOCK with the recently completed coastal minesweeper ALVERTON already renamed THAMES for RNVR duties, while BARBERRY is visible astern.

Lisahally, three miles downstream from Londonderry on the east bank of the River Foyle, had been built as an escort base during WW2. Surrendered U-boats berthed there in 1945 before final disposal. The wooden quay was used as a lay-up berth, best viewed from the river. This rare view on 30 June 1956 shows three Black Swan frigates: STORK (inboard), ALACRITY and the bows of ACTAEON, soon to become the German HIPPER.

Some 200,000 tons of naval vessels were laid up in the Gareloch, including three battleships and two carriers, on 15 July 1956. This view looking north-east towards Faslane shows ANSON (nearest camera), KING GEORGE V (right) and the cruiser SWIFTSURE awaiting her aborted modernisation. The floating dock beyond the latter is BAU 300, her German builder's number at Flenderwerke. The 9500-ton lift capacity dock had been brought from Lübeck to Barrow in 1947, laid up in the Gareloch from 1950. She was towed to Haugesund five days after this photograph was taken.

Most of the RN's big ships were laid up in the Gareloch in the mid 1950s. ILLUSTRIOUS was laid up in 1954 after service as trials carrier. Seen here on 14 April 1956, she was towed (on 3 November 1956) the three miles up the loch to Shipbreaking Industries' Faslane yard. Her near sister INDEFATIGABLE laid up just out of the picture left a day later on 4 November for demolition at Dalmuir.

17

Four of the surviving M class destroyers (on 12 August 1956) at Penarth, across the bay from Cardiff, a redundant coal exporting dock used for Reserve Fleet ships in the 1950s. Outboard is MARNE, then MATCHLESS, MILNE and METEOR. They saw little postwar service, being transferred to Turkey twelve months later, refitted in the UK, and delivered in 1959.

Near the entrance lock at Penarth (on 3 April 1959) are
GUARDIAN and the trawler WIAY. The former had arrived from
Plymouth in 1958 to be refitted by Penarth Pontoon, Slipway &
Ship Repairing Co further up the dock. She was broken up at
Troon in December 1962.

West Bute Dock in Cardiff was 'Death Row' for Hunts in the 1950s. CATTISTOCK and CROOME (outboard) are seen on 12 August 1956. Neither saw postwar service. CROOME still displays her WW2 pendant number L62 on a pinkish coloured hull, although the flag superior had been changed to F in 1947. Four other Hunts are out of view in the dock, now filled in

The west side of East Bute Dock at Cardiff was used by twenty vessels of the South Wales Reserve Fleet, under the HQ ship CAMBRIA (ex DERG). Four of the remaining River class frigates are berthed near to redundant coal loading facilities on 12 August 1956: from left to right JED, ODZANI (a South African river), KALE and TAFF. All but JED went to Cashmore's yard at Newport within ten months, where they yielded about 1130 tons of scrap each, including 90 tons of valuable non-ferrous metal.

HOWE was the only KGV class battleship laid up outside the Gareloch. She is seen at Devonport on 5 August 1957, in Extended Reserve, with coastal minesweeper DARLASTON and MRC 1122 alongside. VANGUARD had shared the same berth a mile north of the Dockyard the previous year before moving to Portsmouth.

Dido class cruisers were laid up at Portsmouth and here at Devonport in the 1950s. EURYALUS, nearest, was the last to pay off, from the South Atlantic in 1954; alongside BELLONA. Beyond them in the Hamoaze on 4 August 1958 are TERPSICHORE and ZEBRA (right)

Two Black Swans show off their riveted shell plating at Barry in South Wales on 11 August 1956. SNIPE lies outboard of PHEASANT, still with a tripod mast. Their guns and directors had recently been 'kooncoted', sprayed with a waterproof coating and dehumidified internally. The white mark on the stem is a telltale to show if the vessel is taking water and sinking more deeply. PHEASANT broke her tow on the way to the breakers at Troon in January 1963, but was recovered. SNIPE realised a net value for BISCO of £14631 from 1054 tons of scrap at Cashmore's Newport yard when demolished in March 1961.

A view along Penarth dock looking east on 3 April 1959, when ten RF ships were left. In the nearest trot are three Castle class frigates, from left to right OXFORD, BAMBOROUGH and KENILWORTH CASTLEs, with Algerine RECRUIT outboard. In the further group are TERPSICHORE in Operational Reserve from Devonport and MRC 1122.

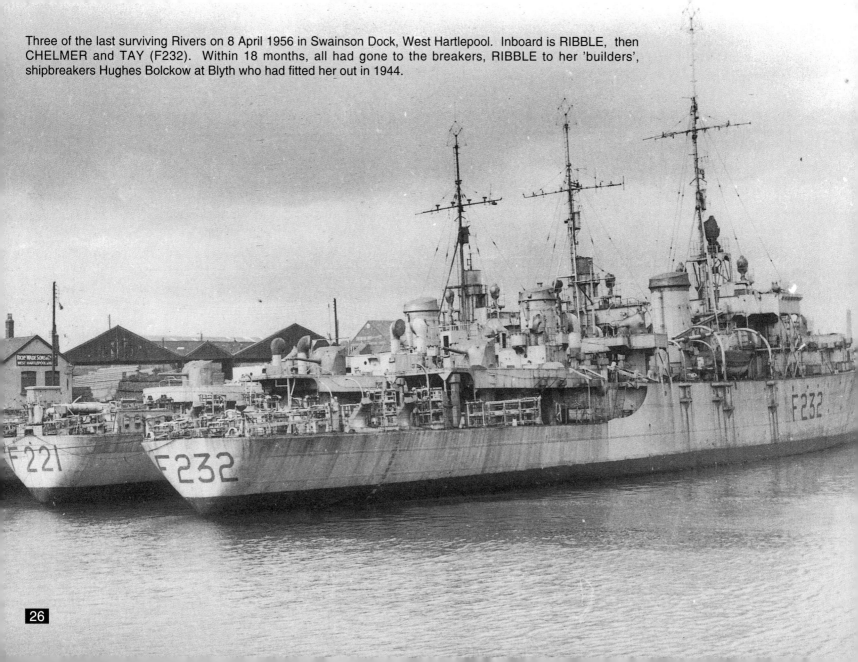

Three of the last surviving Rivers on 8 April 1956 in Swainson Dock, West Hartlepool. Inboard is RIBBLE, then CHELMER and TAY (F232). Within 18 months, all had gone to the breakers, RIBBLE to her 'builders', shipbreakers Hughes Bolckow at Blyth who had fitted her out in 1944.

26

A corner of Jackson Dock at Hartlepool on 18 August 1957. Minesweeper ESPIEGLE, with A/S mortar Squid instead of 4-inch gun, recently refitted at Gray's yard lies on LOCHs MORE and TRALAIG. The SDB to the right is GREATFORD.

Seaward Defence Boats built in the latter half of the 1950s were seen mainly as 'hostilities only' vessels protecting naval bases from submarine attack, so most were kept in reserve after completion, being sold in the mid 1960s. Eight were berthed at Barrow in the Devonshire Dock entrance basin (since filled in) on 4 April 1960. The three in the nearest trot are (L to R) MONTFORD, TILFORD and MARLINGFORD, with HINKSFORD outboard in the next trot. The 40mm Bofors and other equipment are kooncoted.

Vickers-Armstrongs used the west side of Buccleuch Dock at Barrow for fitting out their larger ships, but the east side was used both for Reserve Fleet ships and for laid-up vessels of the Isle of Man Steam Packet Company. Alongside Algerine minesweeper WATERWITCH (on 4 April 1960) are MRC 1015 and MRC 1098, the latter from Hartlepool.

Fareham Creek up Portsmouth Harbour has long been used to berth decommissioned warships. This view looking north (on 12 March 1967) shows the cruiser GAMBIA, with the Type 15 frigate ROCKET alongside about to depart for the breakers at Dalmuir. In the distance are (L to R) the destroyers CROSSBOW, LAGOS and CARRON.

This line of vessels at Portsmouth, also on 12 March 1967, includes the destroyer CASSANDRA (nearest), Type 15 frigate WHIRLWIND, the last Loch to have been in commission LOCH LOMOND and the ex-sonar trials vessel Hunt class BROCKLESBY.

The graveyard south-west corner of Rosyth dockyard basin on 7 July 1957. The former Cunarder AURANIA had been converted to the repair ship ARTIFEX in 1944, then used as an artificers' training ship at Rosyth from 1948. Alongside her is the Hunt class TALYBONT (F118), also used in artificer training, which went for scrap at Charlestown two miles to the west on 14 February 1961. Outboard is the uncompleted hull of a Battle class destroyer to have been named JUTLAND, but known as Job 4922. Her construction was stopped soon after launch on 2 November 1945 at Hawthorn Leslie, although not before her main machinery had been shipped together with her funnel. She was used as a trials vessel by the then newly established Naval Construction Research Establishment (NCRE) in the Forth until scrapped by Shipbreaking Industries at their Rosyth yard, on 11 September 1957. The tanker is the 1916-built PHILOL, then in use as a sullage vessel, receiving fuel oil removed from the bunkers of ships in the dockyard. Outboard is a crane lighter. The bows are of the diving tender DIVER.

POSTWAR SHIPBREAKING

Many of the ships illustrated in this book were broken up under the auspices of the British Iron & Steel Corporation (Salvage) Ltd - normally called just BISCO. The Admiralty usually disposed of surplus ships in peacetime by competitive tender to commercial shipbreakers (if for demolition) or to shipowners/brokers (if for further use), but a different system operated between WW2 and 1962. During the war, government control over raw material supplies for the steel industry such as iron ore and scrap was exercised through the agency of BISCO. Hence salvaged materials and scrap metal suitable for steelmaking were acquired and handled by BISCO and allocated according to various steelworks' needs. Scrap such as from shipbreaking was used as part of the charge for open hearth furnaces producing mild steel and for electric arc furnaces making special steels - the origin of 'ships being turned into razor blades'.

There was very little shipbreaking during WW2, as even the most decrepit ships could be found some use, if only as blockships. BISCO was able to salvage material from wrecks around the UK coast, the actual contractors often being shipbreakers such as Metal Industries. (See "Metal Industries: Shipbreaking at Rosyth and Charlestown" by Ian Buxton; World Ship Society 1992) Thus any surplus government vessels during and after the war were 'handed over' to BISCO, who then arranged the actual demolition by 'allocating' the vessel to a suitable shipbreaker. The latter then demolished the vessel as a subcontractor to BISCO, despatching the ferrous scrap to nearby steelworks and the more valuable non-ferrous metals to specialist merchants. BISCO collected the sale proceeds, paid the shipbreaker his direct demolition costs plus a fee per ton for overheads and profit, and paid for other costs such as towage, carriage and insurance. After deducting its own fee, BISCO returned the surplus to the current government department responsible, which ranged from the Ministry of Supply, the Ministry of Power to the Admiralty. This sum was effectively a deferred 'sale' price paid a year or two afterwards. No money was agreed or changed hands at the time of handover, so reference books describing RN ships as being 'Sold to Breaker X' over this period are incorrect, except for a handful of vessels, usually small.

Thus BISCO would be notified by the Admiralty when a vessel had been approved to scrap. It would then decide on a suitable breaker, based upon: the type, size and draft of the vessel with respect to individual breakers' facilities, the capabilities and current workload in each yard, the distance from the vessel's lay-up berth, and the demand for scrap from the various steelworks - BISCO serving the whole industry even before nationalisation. Postwar, there were around 25 shipbreaking yards, most of them sited within easy rail distance of a steelworks. Only four yards, all in Scotland, were capable of demolishing a battleship or fleet carrier: Ward's at Inverkeithing on the Forth, and three on the Clyde, namely Metal Industries (later Shipbreaking Industries) at Faslane, Arnott Young at Dalmuir, and Arnott Young, later Shipbreaking (Queenborough) at Cairnryan.

BISCO would then arrange towage, either chartering commercial tugs, often from United Towing of Hull, or using Admiralty tugs. Dockyard tugs would be responsible for the unberthing and hand the vessel over to the deep sea tugs. The tow would average around 5 knots, depending on the weather. Thus if the weather was reasonable, the voyage from a south coast dockyard to the Clyde or Forth would take 4-5 days. One tug would be sufficient for a small vessel, but a carrier with its high windage would require up to four. Local tugs would undertake the actual berthing at the shipbreaking yard's wharf, carried out, where possible, on spring tides to give the greatest depth alongside, especially at those yards whose berths dried out at low tide.

Once at the yard, any saleable equipment or furniture would be removed ashore for storage or sale, which helped reduce the fire risk. The ship burners would use oxy-acetylene cutting torches (later oxy-propane) to cut out the largest chunks of superstructure and upper deck that the shore cranes could readily handle. In small yards this might only be via a 5-ton Scotch derrick, but the bigger yards had cranes of around 50 tons capacity. The chunks would then be cut by shore burners into furnace size sections, typically 5 x 2 feet, weighed and loaded into rail wagons. Equipment, piping and cables would first be separated to go to the non-ferrous workshop to be stripped down to recover the brass, copper, gunmetal and lead. Residual oil fuel, insulation and rubbish like tiles from washplaces would be sold or dumped. Good quality timber like teak from the decks was carefully recovered and made into items such as garden furniture. A shed would hold 'reusables' like pumps, generators, winches and furniture, and sometimes steering wheels and bells (though these latter were usually removed from naval vessels before disposal). All such items were sold for much higher prices than plain scrap, either to regular buyers or casual callers.

As the hull was cut down deck by deck, the machinery spaces would be opened up, revealing the overall layout in a way that could not be seen during construction. Thick side and turret armour was usually cut into smaller pieces, rather than separated into their original plates. The nickel content of cemented side armour increased its value two or three times compared with ordinary steel scrap. The strength of the hull was progressively reduced, so care had to be taken to retain the sides of each deck for stiffness, and avoid weight concentrations. The now almost unrecognisable hull floated higher in the water, and was ready to be moved to the finishing berth. The beaching ground 'dried' out at low tide (usually to a glutinous mud requiring stout knee-high boots), which allowed the final sections of double bottom to be removed without worrying about floatation or strength.

The shipbreaker would render all his figures to BISCO, who would then prepare a final account, both of outturn of materials and of costs. A summary of those for a battleship and destroyer are shown.

Howe   35000 tons standard displacement.   Completed 1942
Arrived T W Ward's Inverkeithing yard 4 June 1958. Demolition completed September 1961

	Tons	Av £/ton	£
Steel scrap	19626	11.1	217,848
Armour scrap	11661	18.5	215,943
Non-ferrous	1934	140.2	271,073
Reusables, sundries and oil	765	19.5	14,946
Total sales	**33986**	**21.18**	**719,810**
Demolition costs		4.98	169,388
Towage, carriage etc			69,068
Total costs		7.02	238,456
Surplus		**14.16**	**481,354**

On standard displacement, surplus equates to £13.75 per ton.
Thus if tenders had been sought for the sale of HOWE, and the breaker had correctly estimated the likely outturn, then he could have bid up to £480,000 less his anticipated profit margin. The sales income would then have covered not only demolition costs and purchase price, but hopefully left a reasonable margin for profit.

Cossack   1710 tons standard displacement.   Completed 1945
Arrived T W Ward's Grays yard 2 February 1960. Demolition completed March 1961

	Tons	Av £/ton	£
Steel scrap	1071	11.04	11,821
Non-ferrous	140	177.0	24,777
Reusables, ballast etc	206	18.7	3,845
Total sales	**1417**	**28.54**	**40,443**
Demolition costs		6.44	9,123
Towage, carriage etc			4,105
Total costs		9.34	13,228
Surplus		**19.20**	**27,215**

On standard displacement, surplus equates to £15.92 per ton.
The standard displacement included consumable items such as stores, ammunition, water etc so the saleable light displacement was less than 1710 tons.

The BISCO scheme was wound up in 1962-3, after which the Admiralty, later the Ministry of Defence, would invite tenders for purchase of surplus ships, usually 'as lies', i.e. in whatever condition the ship was, wherever it was lying. The various breakers then had about a month to inspect the ship and prepare their estimates of outturns, sales income and costs, and submit bids. The successful bidder usually had to pay the agreed sale price in full before a

Certificate of Purchase would be issued and the vessel towed away. Although Belgium and Holland had long been buyers of small auxiliary type vessels such as boom defence vessels, until the 1980s British warships were only sold to British breakers. The price they could offer was heavily influenced by the forward price of steel that the British Steel Corporation was prepared to pay.

From about 1980, British yards were handicapped by (a) low scrap prices following a drop in demand from BSC, (b) poor market for reusable equipment (few in Britain wanted to buy secondhand equipment and furniture, while with the rundown of the British merchant navy, there was little demand from shipowners for spare parts), (c) higher wage rates than southern Europe or Indian sub-continent and (d) increasingly demanding health and safety requirements, particularly as regards the handling of asbestos in lagging and insulation. Spain was the first purchaser of a large ship, the repair ship TRIUMPH in 1981, while in the 1990s, it has become economic to tow even small vessels like frigates long distances to India. Thus UK breakers might only be able to offer around half the price an overseas buyer could tender, so the whole industry had shrunk in the mid-1990s to one only employing a few dozen men, compared with the thousands in its heyday after both world wars.

Today's prices are modest, with a destroyer/frigate commanding only around £100,000, under 1% of what it had cost to build after allowing for inflation. Thus there is little financial sacrifice in allowing redundant warships to be used in experiments and sunk as targets. From 1978 onwards when the frigate UNDAUNTED was sunk by torpedo from SWIFTSURE after use as a target vessel, a succession of warships has been expended in trials and exercises.

With such a pattern of disposal and fewer ships in the Royal Navy, the sights such as are illustrated in this book will never be seen again in Britain, unless a decision is made to break up nuclear submarines, as the United States are doing at Puget Sound Naval Shipyard.

(Right) Almost the last big guns of the Royal Navy fall to the cutters torch. This photograph was taken onboard VANGUARD at Faslane in August 1960.

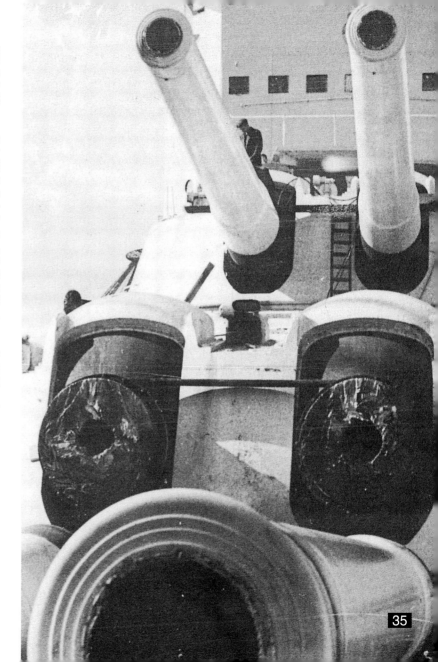

35

IRON DUKE well cut down at Faslane in 1947. The demilitarised battleship had been bomb damaged at Scapa Flow on 17 October 1939, then beached at Longhope as a depot ship for the rest of the war. Refloated on 19 April 1946 by Metal Industries, she became the first ship to be broken up at their newly leased Faslane yard, arriving on 19 August 1946. No.1 Military Port (Faslane) had been completed in 1942 to supplement the Clyde's overstretched dock facilities, hence the cargo handling type cranes on the quay, reportedly removed from bomb damaged Southampton. Her hulk was beached at the Smith & Houston yard at Port Glasgow in November 1948 for final demolition as Faslane's beaching ground had not yet been completed.

RODNEY was the first of four battleships to arrive at Ward's Inverkeithing yard within a 14-month period. Here she has just arrived (on 26 March 1948) at the deep water wharf, berthing outboard of ex-German 11590 GRT liner GENERAL OSORIO, with the stern of ex-German 6390 GRT cargo vessel BELGRANO at the finishing berth to the left. Demolition of RODNEY had already started at Rosyth Dockyard early in 1948 to lighten her to get into Inverkeithing. This included removal of all six twin 6-inch turrets. She was beached on 13 April 1949, with removal of her last sections in December 1949. She yielded a total of 31,763 tons of scrap.

RODNEY at Inverkeithing's deep water wharf on 19 August 1948 showing 'B' triple 16-inch turret, following removal of the seven and a quarter-inch roof plates. The panels on the rear cover are ventilation holes. Ahead of her is British India's cargo liner KARAGOLA, furthest centre the hulk of FRESNO STAR, to the left GENERAL OSORIO. The viaduct carries the main Edinburgh to Aberdeen railway, providing a good view for passengers of the yard.

(Left) RODNEY'S 'X' turret, with most of the 108-ton barrels cut off, on 19 August 1948. The face plates were 16 inches of cemented armour. (Inset) The other end of 'X' turret on the same day, a view never previously seen during construction or service. The left hand gun is lying in its forged steel cradle with hydraulic recoil cylinder, both elevating together. The centre gun reveals the thickness round the breech and some of the wire winding at the forward end of the cut; the 16-inch was the last such British heavy gun so constructed.

NELSON being brought round from Rosyth to Inverkeithing on 15 March 1949, having just passed under the Forth Bridge. She had been lightened to 27ft 6in draught, but still partially grounded at low tide when berthed at Ward's. The vertical lines on her hull show the position of transverse bulkheads, probably indicators from her use as a target for bombing trials in the Forth in the summer of 1948.

(Left) NELSON arrives on 15 March 1949, to berth close to REVENGE. Like RODNEY, around 1500 tons had been removed at Rosyth to lighten her, including all 6-inch turrets and the muzzle sections of the guns in 'B' and 'X' 16-inch triple turrets, and her propellers. (Right) NELSON'S 16-inch director control tower is toppled at Inverkeithing on 31 August 1949. Often awkward heavy items such as masts out of reach of the cranes were felled in this way, then cut up where they lay. Demolition was completed in October 1950, after 33,134 tons had been recovered.

Inverkeithing at its busiest. This view taken on 24 May 1949 shows three battleships, with RODNEY on the finishing berth which dried out at low tide, Nelson at the deep water berth, with REVENGE outboard. Although the latter arrived six months before NELSON, she was not finished until the end of 1952. A new office block is under construction for Ward's next to the road. 1949 was the peak year of British shipbreaking, with around 500,000 tons of scrap produced, the equivalent of sixteen battleships or 400 destroyers. (Aerofilms)

ROYAL SOVEREIGN had been returned as the Soviet ARCHANGELSK at Rosyth in February 1949. Ward's commenced dismantling her in the Forth in June 1949, bringing her into Inverkeithing Bay as seen here on 6 March 1950. All four 15-inch turrets have been removed, part of the 2,882 tons already taken off. The two visible turrets belong to REVENGE moored outboard. She finally yielded over 29,000 tons of scrap.

REVENGE's spotting top and high angle director are felled in 1951. She was the last of the WW1 battleships to reach the steelmaker's furnaces - apart from the bones of WARSPITE on the rocks in Mounts Bay.

The battlecruiser RENOWN, modernised in 1939, arrives at Metal Industries' yard at Faslane on 8 August 1948. She had been towed from Plymouth on 3 August by United Towing's ENGLISHMAN, MASTERMAN and SEAMAN for a price of £5000. The lead tug for the final move up the Gareloch is Steel & Bennie's FORAGER. ENGLISHMAN and SEAMAN then returned to Plymouth to tow VALIANT to Cairnryan.

Two views of cruiser Norfolk at Cashmore's yard at Newport (S Wales) on 14 March 1950. She had arrived from the River Fal in tow of ENGLISHMAN (ex naval tug ENCHANTER 762 GRT/1625 ihp) on 19 February, for which United Towing received £950. The left hand view shows 'Y' turret, 'X' having been removed at her Tyne refit between January and November 1944. (T W Ferrers-Walker)

Submarines with their near cylindrical hulls could lie at awkward angles when beached. U class UTHER demonstrates this propensity at Ward's Hayle yard in Cornwall, having arrived there on 20 February 1950. Her 3-inch gun was still aboard, as were the lead-rich batteries, producing 571 tons of scrap overall.

At Ward's Grays yard on the Thames, S class submarine SPIRIT is wedged against the crumbling Columbia Wharf by coastal escort GUILLEMOT. In the background is the beached hulk of the submarine TRUCULENT, rammed and sunk in the Thames on 12 January 1950. She was salvaged on 14 March and moved to Ward's on 19 June. GUILLEMOT had arrived on 29 June and SPIRIT on 6 July, so the view was probably taken later in July. The site is now a housing estate.

After lying at Spithead awaiting handing over to BISCO, FORMIDABLE was towed away on 7 May 1953 by ENGLISHMAN, TRADESMAN and SEAMAN. She is seen just after berthing at Inverkeithing on 12 May from manager Tom Gray's office window. The foreground shows the typical proceeds of a shipbreaking yard, with steel about to be loaded into wagons, and equipment being stripped down to extract non-ferrous metals, handled by the 5 and 10-ton scotch derricks.

With low height upper and lower 14ft hangars, IMPLACABLE was not worth modernising. Paying off as a training ship in 1954, she lay at Portsmouth until she was towed to Ward's Inverkeithing yard. She is seen on 4 November 1955, one day after arrival, alongside EMPIRE TROOPER. Demolition took 24 months, yielding 23,639 tons, of which 2,510 was classed as rubbish, including insulation, tiling and cement.

HMAS AUSTRALIA leaves Sydney on 26 March 1955, probably the longest tow ever to a British shipbreaking yard. Such was the shortage of scrap in Britain that BISCO was prepared to buy ships on the other side of the world. Smit's tug RODE ZEE finally delivered the cruiser to Ward's Barrow yard on 5 July 1955, a tow of 101 days, averaging 4.8 knots.

The early Dido class cruisers saw little service postwar, all having gone to the breakers by 1959, with CLEOPATRA arriving at Newport on 15 December 1958. Here she is seen on the mud of the River Usk at Cashmore's yard on 7 February 1959. The funnels are already off to start opening up the machinery spaces, sources of valuable non-ferrous metals. The top of her 3-inch armour belt can be seen at upper deck level. Breaking of CLEOPATRA realised a surplus of £82,851 after all demolition costs had been deducted from sales of 5,589 tons of scrap worth £120,144. (T W Ferrers-Walker)

The last of the KGV battleships HOWE arrives at Inverkeithing on 4 June 1958, with Rosyth dockyard tug ENERGY assisting. HOWE had spent an embarrassing day grounded south of the entrance channel on 2 June. Her deep sea tugs, WELSHMAN and ENGLISHMAN, got her off the next day, but fog delayed berthing until the 4th. Demolition started on the 6th.

HOWE safely berthed on 5 June alongside submarine depot ship MONTCLARE (originally a Canadian Pacific liner before conversion in WW2). She was to yield 33,986 tons of material with a net value after demolition costs of £481,354. Amongst equipment removed from the ship and returned to Admiralty stores were: anchors, six single Bofors (the 2-pdr were scrapped with the ship), workshop tools, ice cream plant and the 95-line telephone exchange, earmarked for the cruiser SWIFTSURE then being modernised at Chatham.

Still recognisable five months later on 5 November 1958, HOWE rides higher in the water as materials are removed. Each 120 tons lifted off raised her one inch out of the water. Chemical analysis of her armour plates was carried out, as the price payable reflected the nickel content. Fifteen-inch cemented side armour had about 4.4% nickel, worth over £20 per ton, or double the mild steel scrap price.

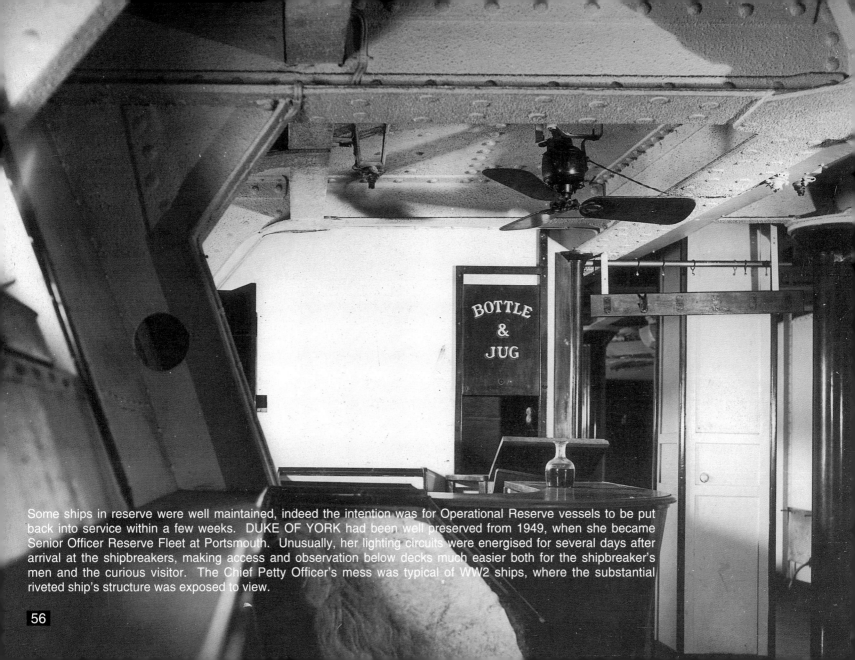

BOTTLE
&
JUG

Some ships in reserve were well maintained, indeed the intention was for Operational Reserve vessels to be put back into service within a few weeks. DUKE OF YORK had been well preserved from 1949, when she became Senior Officer Reserve Fleet at Portsmouth. Unusually, her lighting circuits were energised for several days after arrival at the shipbreakers, making access and observation below decks much easier both for the shipbreaker's men and the curious visitor. The Chief Petty Officer's mess was typical of WW2 ships, where the substantial riveted ship's structure was exposed to view.

ANSON being manoeuvred alongside at Faslane on 17 December 1957. Clyde Shipping's tugs have had to move her only a mile from her mooring buoy in the Gareloch. The hulk at the right is the liner OTRANTO, lying at the berth that is now incorporated into the submarine base HMS NEPTUNE.

ANSON's quarterdeck and 'Y' quadruple 14-inch turret in March 1958, masts and funnels gone. She yielded 35,232 tons of scrap worth £458,170 net. The teak decking was sent down to Blyth where Shipbreaking Industries' sister company Hughes Bolckow made garden furniture.

ANSON's hull shape and form of structure become apparent as top hamper is removed. By 12 August 1958, she has been cut down two decks forward to Middle Deck level. The ring bulkhead supporting the 1550-ton revolving weight of 'A' turret is still intact. The side armour abreast the turret reveals not only the thickness, but the tongue-and-groove joints. Astern lie the hulks of liner ASTURIAS and frigate FLINT CASTLE.

Two shipbreakers operated next to each other on the River Tyne at Gateshead, C W Dorkin and J J King. Seen from the old Redheugh Bridge on 20 June 1962 are minesweepers WELCOME (nearest at Dorkin's) still fitted with her 4-inch gun and WAVE at King's (with Squid) having been used as a fishery protection vessel. The two yards closed soon afterwards once the BISCO scheme had been wound up; no trace of the yards can now be found on the river bank.

Black Swan frigate OPOSSUM partly dried out at Demmelweek & Redding's yard in Sutton Pool, Plymouth on 30 July 1960. The yard's technique of starting from the bow reveals both the hull shape and the structure forward. The section is through the forward twin 4-inch mount, while forward of the lower transverse bulkhead, the Type 144 sonar transducer is just visible. She yielded a net value of £17,674 from 986 tons of scrap.

Reserve Fleet ships arriving at breaker's yards were typically in the condition revealed in these views of Hunt class WHADDON (nearest) and frigate WIGTOWN BAY. The former had arrived at Shipbreaking Industries Clyde yard from Cardiff on 5 April 1959, the latter from Barry on 13 April. Despite WHADDON realising 1010 tons, 192 tons less than the Bay, she yielded a surplus of £24,595, compared with the Bay's £14,436, owing to her much larger weight of non-ferrous from her destroyer type machinery. WHADDON was moved to Faslane's beaching ground for demolition of her lower hull on 11 August, with WIGTOWN BAY following on 3 September.

LARGO BAY at Ward's Inverkeithing yard, only 20 miles west of the real Largo Bay, about February 1959. With the deepwater berth occupied, she has been moved complete to the finishing berth drawing less than 11 ft of water, but 'drying' out at low tide, although that is hardly an accurate description of the glutinous mud that formed the bottom of most beaching grounds.

Red faces all round as battleship VANGUARD, drawing 28 ft forward, grounds at Point when leaving Portsmouth Harbour on 4 August 1960 for breaking up on the Clyde. The dockyard tugs ANTIC (left) and CAPABLE strain to pull her off. She had arrived at Portsmouth in November 1956 to become flagship of the Reserve Fleet.

VANGUARD approaching the Narrows at the entrance to the Gareloch on 8 August 1960. Local tugs have taken over from the deep sea tugs SAMSONIA and ADVICE. Her arrival attracted large crowds, with local boatmen out in force for photographers.

Hand-held oxy-propane cutters did most of the work in British shipbreaking yards. Even 11-inch thick side plates from VANGUARD's 'Y' turret on 4 September 1960 yield to the steady hand of one of Faslane's Polish workers, displaced after WW2. The lifting capacity of the cranes determined the weight of each piece and thus the dimensions of the plate cut. VANGUARD's 'X' turret had originally been destined to be RENOWN's fourth turret before the latter was redesigned in 1915 as a 6-gun battlecruiser; her 'Y' turret would have gone into REPULSE. Both turrets actually went into COURAGEOUS, but were removed when the latter was converted into an aircraft carrier in 1925. Demolition of S.3 and S.4 twin 5.25-inch Mark 2 mounts has yet to start.

VANGUARD's 100-ton 15-inch gun barrels were cut off at the turret face shortly after arrival and removed by shore crane. The heavier breech end awaited removal of the turret roof plates and the positioning of Faslane's 60-ton floating crane outboard. The hoops of the jacket are being cut off like layers of an onion. This end of a 15-inch had two A tubes inside, then 79 layers of wire and an outer jacket, plus the breech ring, giving an overall diameter of 68.5 inches.

Most of the X-craft midget submarines that survived the war were used for experimental purposes afterwards. Some were tested to destruction at NCRE at Rosyth, while others needed the Clyde's deeper waters. One series involved lowering an X-craft from the bows of boom defence vessel BARFOOT until it collapsed from the pressure of water, which helped check design calculations. In another series, charges were detonated alongside a submerged X-craft, with the results being scaled up to correspond to a depth charge against a full size submarine. The mangled remains of two X-craft have been lifted onto the wharf at Faslane at the end of 1946. EXTANT was the unofficial name given to XT.1, but the identity of the bows-in-air craft is uncertain, probably another XT type.

The light fleet carriers which had seen service in the Korean war but not converted or sold abroad had all gone by 1962. GLORY had been laid up at buoys in the Forth since 1957, so had only a few miles to go to her last berth at Inverkeithing on 23 August 1961. She had been fully refitted at Rosyth in 1955-56 at a cost of £568,470, but her scrap value was only about £150,000.

Demolishing a carrier's island when the vessel was port side to the breaker's wharf was always a problem, usually requiring material to be dragged across the flight deck before lifting off. Left shows part of GLORY's compass platform being lifted ashore upside down by Inverkeithing's 50-ton crane, while (right) THESEUS' mast is pulled over by crane and snatch block once most of the legs have been cut through. This photograph was taken in the summer of 1962 at Inverkeithing.

The 60-ton floating crane at Faslane made it easier to remove sections outside the reach or capacity of the shore cranes. A small section of the light fleet carrier OCEAN's bow is removed in the summer of 1962. The crane was built as MOWT 2 in 1942 for use at Liverpool, sold postwar to Metal Industries. The company was renamed Shipbreaking Industries in 1953.

By 1963, the BISCO central purchase scheme had been wound up, with several smaller shipbreakers closing down. The large companies like Shipbreaking Industries bid for small as well as large vessels to fill their yards. Unmodernised T class submarines TUDOR and TRENCHANT were purchased jointly at Portsmouth. The pair arrived in tow on 23 July 1963 on a typical rainy day at Faslane, TUDOR nearest.

Shipbreaking Industries bought three Canadian Tribal class destroyers through a middleman in New York, their original purchaser having been Marine Salvage Ltd of Port Colborne. All three had paid off at Halifax early in 1964. The price was a lump sum of £132,000 delivered Faslane, so that the sellers had to arrange towage from Halifax. NOOTKA (inboard) arrived on 22 September 1964 in tow of ROBBENPLATE, CAYUGA (in background) arrived on 30 September in tow of ROTESAND, and MICMAC (outboard) arrived on 14 October, just before this picture was taken.

Several small shipbreakers have operated on the Medway since the 1960s to the present day. Shipbreaking (Queenborough) Ltd was backed by local scrap merchants, using the Washer Wharf at Queenborough near Sheerness. The minesweeper CHEERFUL is shown being used as a storage barge on 24 July 1965, until enough scrap has been stockpiled for a shipload to be exported to Spain. Some of the sections are from Capt Johnny Walker's famous sloop STARLING, lying almost invisible at the outer berth, astern of the coaster.

(Opposite Page) The 6-inch cruiser MAURITIUS alongside Ward's Inverkeithing yard shortly after her arrival from Portsmouth on 27 March 1965, purchased for £231,000. Very little equipment has been stripped; the Admiralty usually gave the shipbreakers a separate de-equipping contract if they wished weapons, reusable equipment and spares to be returned to their stores depots.

(This Page Top) About a month after her arrival, MAURITIUS' fore funnel has been lifted off complete, prior to cutting to smaller sizes for the furnaces. (Bottom) One of her twin 4-inch Mark XIX high angle mounts, lifted off complete at around 15 tons weight. By now the monitor ROBERTS had taken her place at the deepwater jetty behind, whose gun barrels are just visible.

The Royal Navy's last 15-inch armed vessel finally succumbs to the demolition men. The 15-inch turret had been removed from the WW1 monitor MARSHAL SOULT in 1940 and shipped to Clydebank for installation in the hull of the new monitor ROBERTS. She had survived as turret drill ship, accommodation ship and fender vessel at Devonport for 20 years. She was towed from there on 19 July 1965 by TYPHOON and SAMSONIA, but had to wait two weeks to berth at Inverkeithing, as it was Ward's annual holiday. Seen alongside MAURITIUS on 4 August, her demolition started on the 20th. Ward's paid £152,600 for her, recovering 7,042 tons of material including 2,264 tons of armour from hull and turret.

Arnott, Young & Co Ltd were significant buyers of redundant warships post-BISCO, a dozen going to them in the first five years. 1950s style anti-submarine vessels were being replaced by the new helicopter-armed Leanders by the mid-1960s, so Type 15 and 16 frigates and ex-Persian Gulf Lochs were disposed of. This line-up at Dalmuir on the Clyde on 15 January 1966 shows (L to R) LOCH VEYATIE, TUMULT and TERMAGANT, representing a purchase cost of £115,000. The basin with its 150-ton crane was originally built by Beardmore at its new Naval Construction Works in 1905 and used for fitting-out until the shipyard closed in 1931.

This unique view of fast minelayer ARIADNE at Dalmuir on 12 May 1965 has to be held at an angle to get the best perspective, but reveals a view that can never have been seen before, not even during construction. The four tracks of the mine deck (one deck below the upper deck) complete with turntables and crossover aft could hold 156 mines. The two inner tracks stopped short of the machinery spaces, whose construction is also revealed. The holes in the aft bulkhead are where each pair of high pressure and low pressure turbines connect to the port and starboard gearboxes in the gearing room. The foremost compartment is the after boiler room, with part of the boiler wall visible.

Fine views of ships breaking up at Dalmuir could be obtained from the cantilever of the 150-ton fitting out crane - by those with a head for heights! The Thornycroft-designed Type 4 Hunt class destroyer BRISSENDEN reveals her lines with their prominent knuckle forward. The three opened compartments on 13 August 1965 are from aft to forward: gearing room, engine room and after boiler room. The 30-ton travelling crane and the row of buildings in the left background had been part of the original Beardmore shipyard (outfitting shops and smithy), but the darker buildings to the right were erected when Dalmuir basin became an outfitting base for newly launched escorts and landing ships in 1943.

Different submarine classes .... and different shapes. Left shows the 1120-ton A-class AMBUSH at Inverkeithing on 23 September 1971 with her saddle tank external water ballast tanks, giving high reserve buoyancy for Pacific duties. She is alongside the frigate WAKEFUL; outboard are AMPHION and ALARIC. All three submarines were purchased at Rosyth by Ward for £92,000, yielding an average of 1,013 tons of scrap each.

Right shows the 780-ton high test peroxide unarmed experimental submarine EXPLORER being demolished at Barrow on 15 August 1965. This view is looking aft, the nearest compartment in the slender high speed hull being the control room, the next two long compartments being the motor room and turbine room. Ward's bought her for only £13,500, surely a bargain given the amount of non-ferrous metal in a submarine.

SHEFFIELD was the last of the Town class cruisers to be scrapped, having been used by the Senior Officer Reserve Fleet at Portsmouth since 1960. After de-equipping at Rosyth early in 1967 (including removal of her 6-inch barrels) she was offered for sale. Shipbreaking Industries' bid of £170,000 was successful. She arrived at Faslane on 22 September 1967, being seen here on the 27th. Mastheads provided good vantage points for photographs, provided that the ladders had not been too heavily corroded by funnel gases and salt spray. She produced 8,154 tons worth £371,011, representing a profit of £93,767 after all costs.

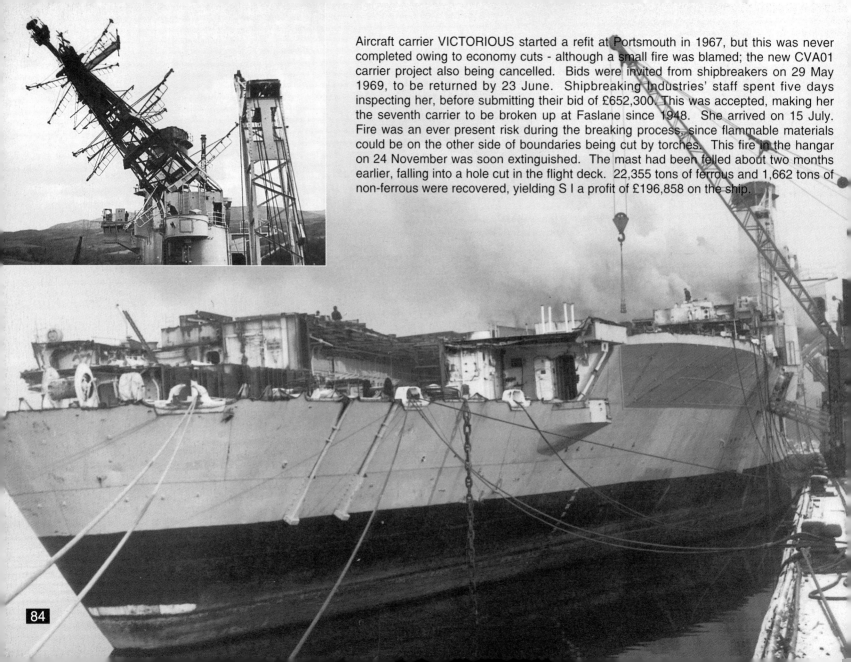

Aircraft carrier VICTORIOUS started a refit at Portsmouth in 1967, but this was never completed owing to economy cuts - although a small fire was blamed; the new CVA01 carrier project also being cancelled. Bids were invited from shipbreakers on 29 May 1969, to be returned by 23 June. Shipbreaking Industries' staff spent five days inspecting her, before submitting their bid of £652,300. This was accepted, making her the seventh carrier to be broken up at Faslane since 1948. She arrived on 15 July. Fire was an ever present risk during the breaking process, since flammable materials could be on the other side of boundaries being cut by torches. This fire in the hangar on 24 November was soon extinguished. The mast had been felled about two months earlier, falling into a hole cut in the flight deck. 22,355 tons of ferrous and 1,662 tons of non-ferrous were recovered, yielding S I a profit of £196,858 on the ship.

It was often easiest to detach entire components for subsequent demolition ashore, rather than cut up piecemeal at the ship. Left shows the frigate CARISBROOKE CASTLE's 4-inch Mark XXIII mount with rocket launcher guides at Faslane on 5 August 1958 (Photo T W Ferrers-Walker). Right shows both funnel and mast being removed from the frigate ULSTER at Inverkeithing in January 1981.

NCRE conducted trials on redundant warships in the Forth, including testing shock resistance and protective systems for both hulls and warheads. After such trials the Weapon class destroyer BROADSWORD shows her mangled stern at Inverkeithing's beaching ground wharf on 14 October 1968. Inboard is the frigate ROEBUCK and ahead the boom defence vessel BARBICAN.

BROADSWORD's detached stern section with its two 10.5 ft diameter 4.5 ton propellers after being raised; delivered by salvage vessel on 7 October 1969. Bronze propellers were among the most valuable scrap items, being worth at that time over £300 per ton compared with about £12 per ton for steel. They were usually sold back to their manufacturers for remelting.

The netlayer PROTECTOR was built in 1936 but was converted into an Antarctic patrol vessel in 1955, being replaced by ENDURANCE in 1967. She was sold to Ward's for £90,600, and is seen arriving at Inverkeithing on 16 March 1970.

The submarine depot ship ADAMANT was in almost continuous service postwar, at Rothesay, Faslane (1957-62) and then Devonport. She was offered for sale in 1966, but not finally sold to shipbreakers until 1970. Ward's were the successful bidder at £171,000. She arrived at Inverkeithing on 11 September 1970, berthed outboard of the destroyer AISNE which arrived on 26 June. From her standard displacement of 12,700 tons, 11,460 tons of saleable material were recovered worth £338,903, including 1,192 tons of armour over magazine and machinery spaces. After demolition costs of £109,793, a profit of £58,110 was realised.

Sunderland had been a shipbreaking port since the end of WW1 until Young's closed in 1963. However in 1974 a berth was leased in Hudson Dock by H Kitson Vickers, a Sheffield firm, who had operated at several different locations post-BISCO. Two Battle class radar picket destroyers are seen on 19 December from the top of the now demolished coal staith, AGINCOURT (inboard) and CORUNNA.

By the 1970s, Ward's once numerous shipbreaking 'depots' had been reduced to three - Inverkeithing, Grays on the Thames and Briton Ferry in South Wales. The Whitby class frigate TENBY is shown at the latter yard in the pill off the River Neath at Giants Grave. She had arrived in tow of ROYSTERER from Devonport on 15 September 1977. Her sellers were actually the Pakistan Navy who had bought her together with SCARBOROUGH with modernisation in mind; the Ministry of Defence only acted as agents for her sale at £82,000.

Cairnryan in south-west Scotland had been built as No. 2 Military Port in WW2, then briefly used for shipbreaking from 1948-50. That activity resumed in 1969, the Government having sold off the port area. It was leased by Shipbreaking (Queenborough) Ltd, who eventually bought the port. Its deepwater jetty was suitable for aircraft carriers outside, with coasters loading the resulting scrap on the inside. From 1972 onwards, CENTAUR, BULWARK, EAGLE and ARK ROYAL were all dismantled there. This view on 30 August 1979 taken from EAGLE's upper hangar deck level looking aft into the lower hangar gives an idea of her construction.

The Whitby class frigate EASTBOURNE had replaced the Type 15 frigate RAPID as training vessel at Rosyth from 1973, initially seagoing, then static in harbour. T W Ward Ltd had been taken over by RTZ in 1982, with the Inverkeithing yard being sold to James A White Ltd, so it was this latter firm that bought EASTBOURNE. She arrived from Rosyth on 7 March 1985, but demolition was spasmodic over the next five years, with the company concentrating on land scrap. She is shown here, cut back to her 4.5-inch gunbay, on 20 May 1988.

By the 1990s, shipbreaking in the UK had almost disappeared in the face of better prices offered by Asian shipbreakers and increasingly onerous health and safety legislation. A rare sight was offered on 6 April 1991 at Millom near Barrow with two Leanders high and reasonably dry, EURYALUS nearest with propellers removed, AURORA bows on. Devonport Management Ltd had acquired the vessels so that spares and equipment could be removed for Leanders in service with other navies. They were 'parked' at Duddon Valley Shipbreakers in the autumn of 1990, but AURORA was not actually broken up until 1992 while demolition of EURYALUS was not completed until 1995.

Low scrap prices...health and safety legislation.....and a requirement to test new weapons saw the frigate LOWESTOFT sunk by a newly modified Mk24 Mod2 Tigerfish torpedo fired by the nuclear powered submarine CONQUEROR in 1986.

INDEX